¡VEO VEO!

VEO V...

# DINERO

MARIE ROESSER

**Gareth Stevens**
PUBLISHING

TRADUCIDO POR
DIANA OSORIO

conceptos
básicos

# ¡Veo dinero!

Veo monedas.

 veinticinco

diez centavos

 cinco centavos

un centavo

Veo un centavo.

Veo una moneda
de cinco centavos.

Veo una moneda
de diez centavos.

Veo una moneda de veinticinco centavos.

Veo un centavo.

Veo una moneda
de cinco centavos.

17

Veo una moneda
de diez centavos.

Veo una moneda de veinticinco centavos.

¡Veo un dólar!

**Please visit our website, www.garethstevens.com. For a free color catalog of all our high-quality books, call toll free 1-800-542-2595 or fax 1-877-542-2596.**

**Library of Congress Cataloging-in-Publication Data**
Names: Roesser, Marie, author.
Title: Veo veo dinero / Marie Roesser.
Description: New York : Gareth Stevens Publishing, [2022] | Series: ¡Veo veo!
  | Includes index.
Identifiers: LCCN 2020013442 | ISBN 9781538267912 (library binding) | ISBN
  9781538267899 (paperback) | ISBN 9781538267905 (6 Pack) | ISBN 9781538267929
  (ebook)
Subjects: LCSH: Money–Juvenile literature. | Mathematics–Study and
  teaching (Elementary)–Juvenile literature.
Classification: LCC HG221.5 .R64 2022 | DDC 332.4–dc23
LC record available at https://lccn.loc.gov/2020013442

First Edition

Published in 2022 by
**Gareth Stevens Publishing**
111 East 14th Street, Suite 349
New York, NY 10003

Translator: Diana Osorio
Editor, Spanish: Rossana Zúñiga
Designer: Katelyn E. Reynolds
Editor: Rossana Zúñiga

Photo credits: Cover, p. 1 FabrikaSimf/Shutterstock.com; cover, back cover, p. 1 (blue background) Irina Adamovich/Shutterstock.com; p. 3 Gavin Kingcome Photography/The Image Bank/Getty Images Plus; pp. 5–21 TokenPhoto/E+/Getty Images; p. 23 (dollar bill) Westend61/Getty Images; p. 23 (coins) Michael Cogliantry/The Image Bank/Getty Images Plus.

Printed in the United States of America

Some of the images in this book illustrate individuals who are models. The depictions do not imply actual situations or events.

CPSIA compliance information: Batch #CWGS22: For further information contact Gareth Stevens, New York, New York at 1-800-542-2595.

Find us on